LOVE OR MONEY?

Are you a good detective? Yes? If you are, then you must find the killer before Inspector Walsh. Inspector Walsh is a police detective; he works slowly, but very carefully. Are you quicker?

What does a detective do? A detective looks for clues. A clue is something, big or small, that tells you who the killer is. Clues are not easy to find, but there are many clues in this story. Some clues are good – they help you. Other clues are bad – they stop you finding the killer. You must read carefully, or you will miss the clues.

But remember: you must not believe everything that people say. The killer will obviously lie. Perhaps other people will also lie, for different reasons. And perhaps they *want* someone to die. But who wants . . . and kills? Can you find the killer?

D0707180

OXFORD BOOKWORMS LIBRARY

Crime & Mystery

Love or Money?

Stage 1 (400 headwords)

Series Editor: Jennifer Bassett
Founder Editor: Tricia Hedge
Activities Editors: Jennifer Bassett and Alison Baxter

ROWENA AKINYEMI

Love or Money?

OXFORD UNIVERSITY PRESS

OXFORD
UNIVERSITY PRESS

Great Clarendon Street, Oxford OX2 6DP

Oxford University Press is a department of the University of Oxford.
It furthers the University's objective of excellence in research, scholarship,
and education by publishing worldwide in

Oxford New York

Auckland Cape Town Dar es Salaam Hong Kong Karachi
Kuala Lumpur Madrid Melbourne Mexico City Nairobi
New Delhi Shanghai Taipei Toronto

With offices in

Argentina Austria Brazil Chile Czech Republic France Greece
Guatemala Hungary Italy Japan Poland Portugal Singapore
South Korea Switzerland Thailand Turkey Ukraine Vietnam

OXFORD and OXFORD ENGLISH are registered trade marks of
Oxford University Press in the UK and in certain other countries

ISBN 978 0 19 478908 0

A complete recording of this Bookworms edition of
Love or Money? is available in an audio pack ISBN 978 0 19 478876 2

Printed in China

ACKNOWLEDGEMENTS
Illustrated by: David Lloyd

Word count (main text): 6010 words

For more information on the Oxford Bookworms Library,
visit www.oup.com/elt/gradedreaders

CONTENTS

Chapter 1

The Clarkson family lived in the country near Cambridge, about half a mile from the nearest village and about a mile from the river. They had a big, old house with a beautiful garden, a lot of flowers and many old trees.

One Thursday morning in July, Jackie came in from the garden. She was a tall, fat woman, thirty years old. It was the hottest day of the year, but she wore a warm brown skirt and yellow shirt. She went into the kitchen to get a drink of water. Just then the phone rang.

'Cambridge 1379,' Jackie said.

The Clarkson family had a big, old house with a beautiful garden.

'Hello. This is Diane. I want to talk to Mother.'

'Mother isn't here,' Jackie said. 'She's at the doctor's.'

'Why? What's wrong?'

'Nothing's wrong,' Jackie said. 'Why are you telephoning? You *are* going to come this weekend? Mother wants everyone to be here.'

'Yes, I want to come,' Diane said. 'I'm phoning because I have no money for the train ticket.'

'No money! Mother is always giving you money!'

'This phone call is very expensive,' Diane said coldly. 'Tell Mother please. I need the money.'

Jackie put the phone down. She took a cigarette from her bag and began to smoke. She felt angry because her sister always asked for money. Diane was twenty years old, the youngest in the family. She lived in London, in one room of a big house. She wanted to be a singer. She sang very well but she could never get work.

Jackie went back into the kitchen and began to make some sandwiches. Just then the back door opened, and her mother came in.

'It's very hot!' Molly said. She took off her hat and put it down on the table. She was a tall, dark woman with beautiful eyes.

Two big, black dogs came into the kitchen after her and ran across to her. She sat down and put her hands on their heads.

'Mother,' Jackie said, 'Diane phoned. She wants money . . .'

Jackie put the sandwiches on the table. 'Mother,' she said, 'Diane phoned. She wants money for her train ticket.'

Molly closed her eyes for a minute. Then she stood up. 'This afternoon I want you to get the house ready for the weekend,' she said. 'Oh, and please go to the village later and get my tablets.'

'Yes, Mother,' Jackie said.

Molly went to the door.

'Mother, please wait a minute,' Jackie said. 'Peter Hobbs came here this morning. He's very angry with you about that letter. He lost his job, you know. Why did you write to his office? He wants to talk to you about it.'

'Well, I don't want to talk to him,' Molly said. She opened the door.

'But Mother, you don't understand. He's seventeen, and it was his first job. He's very, very angry. He says . . . he says he's going to kill you!'

Molly did not answer. She went out of the room and closed the door.

Chapter 2

It was seven o'clock on Saturday evening. Jackie stood at the window. A car drove slowly up to the front door and stopped. A tall man with white hair got out. It was Albert, the husband of Molly's sister.

'Here's Uncle Albert,' Jackie said. 'Always late.'

She went out of the room and opened the front door. Albert came in and went at once to Molly.

'Oh, dear. I'm very late. I *am* sorry,' Albert said. 'Fifty years old today! What a wonderful dress!'

Molly did not smile. 'Thank you, Albert. We're all getting older.' Tonight she wore a long black dress, and the two black dogs sat at her feet. 'Everyone is here now. Let's go in to dinner,' she said.

Everyone stood up and went to the table.

'The table looks nice, Jackie. What wonderful flowers!' Diane said. She was a beautiful girl, with long

'*The table looks nice, Jackie. What wonderful flowers!*' Diane said.

black hair and dark blue eyes. She wore a long red dress.

Albert sat down next to Roger. Roger was Molly's son, her second child. He lived in Cambridge, in an expensive house.

'Someone called Peter stopped me down the road,' Albert said. 'Who is he? He's very angry with you, Molly.'

'That's Peter Hobbs, from the house across the road,' Jackie said quickly. She looked across the table at Molly. 'He lost his job last week and he's angry with everyone.'

'It's Molly he doesn't like,' Albert said.

Molly said nothing. Everyone began to eat.

'How is Aunt Annie?' Jackie asked.

'She's much worse now,' Albert said. 'She stays in bed all the time. She needs a nurse twenty-four hours a day.'

'I am sorry,' Molly said.

Albert stopped eating and looked at Molly. 'It's very difficult and very expensive, you know. Annie feels very unhappy because you don't visit her, Molly. She loves you very much. You are her little sister, you know.'

Molly closed her eyes for a minute. 'I know that, Albert. I am fifty years old, but I am always her "little" sister. Well, we can talk about it later.'

Albert laughed. 'Oh yes, we can talk later. It's always later with you, Molly. Always tomorrow. Never today.'

Jackie watched her mother. Her mother was angry with Albert. Molly never liked talking about her sister Annie and she did not like visiting her because she was very ill.

'That's a beautiful dress, Diane. Is it new?' Jackie asked.

'Thank you, Jackie. Yes, it's new, and very expensive. I got it on Wednesday,' Diane said. She smiled at Jackie.

'All your things are expensive,' Jackie said. She remembered the phone call on Thursday about the train ticket.

'I don't like cheap things,' Diane said. 'And I'm going to need more money soon. I want to go to America. Can you help me, Roger?'

'Oh no,' Roger said. 'Nobody wants to help you, Diane. You don't like working, we all know that, but we all want you to get a job.'

Diane laughed. 'It doesn't matter, Roger. I don't need your help. Mother always helps me. Mother loves me best.' She suddenly smiled, a quick, beautiful smile. But her eyes were cold.

Jackie looked at her mother. Molly's face was white. Jackie did not understand. Was her mother afraid of

Diane said: 'Mother always helps me. Mother loves me best.'

Diane? Jackie wanted her mother to be happy today.

'Would you like some more meat, Uncle Albert?' Jackie asked. 'Roger, can you give everyone some more to drink?'

Roger got up and began to give more wine to everyone. 'This is good wine,' he said.

Molly smiled for the first time. 'Yes, your father loved this wine. He often drank it.'

'Yes,' Albert said, and looked at Molly. 'Expensive, too.'

'Would you like to meet Mr Briggs this weekend, Roger?' Jackie asked quickly. 'He's the new man at the farm. He wants to meet you.'

'Briggs? Briggs?' Molly said, suddenly angry. 'Don't

talk to me about that man. I don't like him. He wants half my garden for his farm. He needs more land, he says. I don't want him in my house. He's always dirty and he has bad teeth.'

Jackie stood up and got her bag. 'Excuse me, I want a cigarette.'

'Cigarettes! Always a cigarette in your mouth,' Molly said. 'I don't like it. Cigarettes aren't good for you.'

Jackie began to smoke. She felt angry but she said nothing. She wanted her mother to be happy this evening, but it was very difficult.

Roger drank some more wine. 'Well, Mother, perhaps Mr Briggs is right. The garden is very big, you know,' he said. 'It's a lot of work for you. The house is big, too. You're fifty now. You need to be more careful.'

'Roger! I don't need a nurse, you know! I work in the garden every day; I feel happy there.' Molly stood up. 'I know you all want my money. You come here for a free dinner, you don't want to see me. You don't love me. You want my house, and my money. Well, you can all wait. Nobody is getting more money from me, not before I die!'

'Don't say that, Mother!' Jackie cried.

Molly walked across the room to the door. 'I feel ill now. I'm going upstairs to bed.'

'*Nobody is getting more money from me, not before I die.*'

Molly left the room. Nobody moved.

'One day I'm going to kill that woman,' Diane said quietly.

Roger looked at Diane but said nothing. Albert moved his head slowly up and down. 'Ill! She's angry, that's all,' he said. 'Molly always gets angry about money. Why can't she be good to her sister? Annie's going to die soon. Molly knows that.'

Jackie finished her cigarette and stood up. 'Would everyone like some coffee? Come into the kitchen and let's drink it there.'

Chapter 3

Early next morning the house was quiet. Suddenly there was a cry from the room next to Roger's, his mother's room. Roger opened his eyes and looked at the clock. It was nearly seven o'clock. He got out of bed and opened the door quietly. At the same time the door of his mother's room opened and Diane came out. Her face was very white.

'Roger! It's Mother! I brought a cup of coffee for her and I found her dead. She's dead . . . dead in her bed,' she cried.

Roger went quickly to the door of his mother's room and looked in. The window was open but the room was warm. Molly was on the bed, one hand under her head. Roger went across to the bed and put his hand on her arm. It was cold. On the little table next to the bed was a hot cup of coffee and an empty cup.

'I'm going to call the doctor,' Diane said.

'She's dead,' Roger said slowly. His face, too, was white. 'Mother is dead!'

Diane walked across the room to the door. 'I'm going to phone the doctor,' she said again.

'Wait a minute!' Roger called. 'Let's tell the family first.'

'She's dead,' Roger said slowly. 'Mother is dead!'

'Family! Nobody loved Mother!' Diane went out and ran downstairs.

Roger slowly went downstairs after her and stood by the telephone.

'Dr Pratt, this is Diane Clarkson. It's my mother – she's dead. Can you come quickly?'

Diane put the phone down. 'It isn't true, Roger! Mother dead! Daddy died last winter, and now Mother.' Diane began to cry.

'Don't cry, Diane,' Roger said. 'Let's go upstairs and tell Uncle Albert and Jackie.'

'No! *You* tell them! Nobody loved Mother. You aren't sorry. Look at you! You want her money. That's all.'

Roger suddenly wanted to hit Diane. 'Be quiet!' he said. 'What about you? You didn't love Mother. You wanted her money, too. Don't forget that!'

'It's true,' Diane said. 'Oh, I can't stay in this house. I'm going out. I'm going to the river with the dogs.'

'No,' Roger said. 'The doctor's coming and I want you here.'

Diane said nothing. She went into the kitchen and at once the dogs got up and came to her. 'Beautiful dogs! Daddy loved you and Mother loved you. Now I'm going to love you.' She opened the back door and went out with the dogs.

Roger did not move. He stood by the telephone. 'It's

true,' he thought. 'I *am* happy about the money. I needed money, and now I'm rich. Things are going to be easier for me now. But Mother . . . why didn't I love her more? And now she's dead.' Slowly, Roger went back upstairs. He wanted to dress before Dr Pratt arrived.

Dr Pratt was a little fat man without much hair. He was the family doctor and he knew all the Clarkson family very well. He went upstairs at once and looked at Molly's body. He looked carefully at the cup of coffee and the empty cup on the table next to her bed.

'I'm sorry, Roger,' he said. 'Where is Diane? She phoned me.'

'She went out with the dogs,' Roger said. 'She was angry with me – angry with everyone.'

Dr Pratt said nothing for a minute. 'This is going to be very difficult. I'm going to phone the police, Roger.'

'Police! Why? What's wrong?'

'I don't know. Your mother wasn't ill. I saw her on Thursday and she was very well. Why did she die? I don't understand. I want to find out.'

Roger went across to the window and looked out at the garden. It was a beautiful summer morning. The sky was blue and the garden was green. It was all very quiet. His mother loved this garden. But Tom Briggs wanted the garden. And Roger wanted the garden, too. Roger felt worse and worse.

Dr Pratt said, 'Why did she die? I don't understand.'

'Your mother took sleeping tablets,' Dr Pratt said. 'Did you know? On Thursday she had a new bottle of tablets, but I can't find it here in her room.'

'I didn't know,' Roger said. 'Very well. Let's go downstairs and you can phone the police.'

Roger went into the kitchen and made some coffee. Just then Diane came in with the dogs.

'Roger,' she said. 'Look, I'm sorry. I was angry and said some angry things.'

'It doesn't matter,' Roger said. 'Here you are, have some coffee. Dr Pratt is phoning the police. Did you know Mother took sleeping tablets? Well, the bottle is not in her room.'

'What? I don't understand.' Diane took the coffee

and began to drink. Her eyes looked big and dark.

Just then Dr Pratt came into the kitchen. 'They're coming at once,' he said. 'Diane – I'm sorry about your mother.'

'Dr Pratt, I want to tell you about last night. Everyone was very angry . . .'

'Be quiet!' Roger said quickly.

'Diane never thinks before she opens her mouth,' he thought angrily.

Diane did not look at Roger. 'Last night Mother went to bed early because everyone . . .'

'Don't tell me,' Dr Pratt said. 'You can tell the police.'

Roger's face went red. Suddenly he felt afraid. 'The police are going to talk to everyone, and ask questions,' he thought. 'And they're going to want answers. It's going to be very difficult.' He finished his coffee and stood up.

'I'm going upstairs,' he said. 'I'm going to tell Uncle Albert and Jackie about Mother . . . and about the police.'

Chapter 4

The police arrived very quickly. There were a lot of them. Some of them with cameras went upstairs to Molly's room. Two detectives talked to Dr Pratt in the kitchen. The family waited in the sitting room. It was a hot day again and the windows were open. The dogs sat quietly at Diane's feet. Nobody talked. Jackie smoked. They waited for a long time. Suddenly the door opened and the two detectives came in.

'Good morning. I am Detective Inspector Walsh and this is Sergeant Foster.' The Inspector did not smile. He

A lot of police arrived very quickly.

was a big man in an old black suit and a black hat and coat. He wore a coat because he always felt cold. 'Last night someone put sleeping tablets in Mrs Clarkson's hot milk. We are going to question everybody, and we need a room, please.'

Roger stood up. 'I'm Roger Clarkson. You can have my father's old office. Come with me, it's along here.'

The office was not a very big room, but there was a table and three or four chairs. Roger opened the window.

'I would like to talk first to your uncle, Albert King,' Inspector Walsh said. He took off his hat and coat and sat down behind the table.

'Of course,' said Roger and left the room.

Sergeant Foster waited by the door. He was a very tall young man with black hair and a nice smile. He was not very happy this morning because he usually played tennis on Sunday mornings. He was one of the best players at the Cambridge Tennis Club.

Albert came in and sat down.

'I'm going to ask some questions, Mr King,' the Inspector said, 'and Sergeant Foster is going to write it all down.'

Albert looked at his feet. 'Yes, yes. It's your job. I know that.'

'Tell me about last night,' Inspector Walsh asked quietly. 'You were angry with Mrs Clarkson.'

'*Sergeant Foster is going to write it all down.*'

Albert looked at Inspector Walsh for the first time. 'Yes, I was. Everyone was angry. Roger was angry. Diane wanted money to go to America. Then there's a man called Tom Briggs . . . He wants half the garden for his farm. Molly was a rich woman. I need money because my wife Annie – Molly's sister – is very ill. I told Molly this.'

'What happened next?'

'Well, Molly was angry with everyone and went upstairs. We went into the kitchen for coffee. Jackie wanted everyone to go up and say good night to Molly. She lives here with Molly so she wanted Molly to be happy. At first Roger said no. He was angry and didn't want to see his mother.'

'And did you see Molly in her room?'

'Yes. I was tired and I went upstairs first. I went to Molly's room and asked her for money again. But no – there was no money for her sister.' Albert stopped and put his hand over his eyes.

Inspector Walsh watched Albert for a minute. 'Did you hear noises after you went to bed?'

'Everyone went into Molly's room to say good night, I think. Later, I heard someone . . . He – or she – went downstairs. That was about midnight.'

'Very well, Mr King. Thank you, you can go now.' Albert left the room.

Inspector Walsh put his hands behind his head.

'What time is it? I'm hungry. We're learning a lot, but I need some coffee.'

'Shall I go to the kitchen?' Sergeant Foster asked.

'Oh, no. Later. Let's see Jackie Clarkson next.'

Jackie came in and sat down. She looked down at her hands and said nothing.

'We found the empty bottle of your mother's sleeping tablets in Diane's room,' the Inspector said suddenly. Then he waited. Jackie's face did not change and she said nothing. 'Tell me, did your mother get her tablets from the shop in the village?'

'Yes. My mother usually took a sleeping tablet every night so she needed a lot of tablets. Sometimes she got

'We found the empty bottle of sleeping tablets in Diane's room.'

them from the shop, sometimes I did. On Thursday, I asked Peter Hobbs to get them. He lives in the house across the road, and he often goes to the village on his bicycle.'

'I see. Your mother wanted to stay in this house. How about you? Did you want to move?'

Jackie looked up for a minute and then down at her hands again. 'This is Mother's house. I loved my mother. She was good to me.'

'Did you see your mother in her room last night?'

'Yes, everyone did. Diane made hot milk and took it to Mother. She usually drank a cup of hot milk before she slept.'

Inspector Walsh put his hands behind his head. Jackie was very quiet. 'What did your mother say?'

Jackie opened her bag and looked for a cigarette. 'Can I smoke?'

'Of course. This is your house,' Inspector Walsh said. He watched Jackie. 'What did your mother say?' he asked again.

'She wanted to go downstairs again. She remembered the dogs – she wanted to get some dinner for them. I went to my room and she went downstairs.'

'What time was this?'

'I don't remember. About midnight, I think.'

'And the cup of hot milk?'

'It was on the table by her bed.'

'Did you need your mother's money?'

'No, Inspector. Money is not important to me. There are more important things,' Jackie said quietly.

'Well, your uncle Albert wanted money. Tom Briggs wanted the garden. You wanted nothing?'

Jackie finished her cigarette and looked up at the Inspector. Her eyes were suddenly angry. 'Don't forget Peter Hobbs. He lost his job because of my mother. He wanted to kill her, you know. And what about Diane? You found the empty bottle in her bag.'

Inspector Walsh listened carefully. 'We're going to question everyone, Miss Clarkson.'

Jackie said nothing for a minute. 'Would you like some sandwiches and coffee, Inspector?'

'Ah! Yes, please!' Inspector Walsh said warmly. 'I would like sandwiches and coffee very much.'

Jackie left the room. Inspector Walsh thought about her. Why was she suddenly angry? The room was quiet.

Chapter 5

After the coffee and sandwiches, Inspector Walsh called Roger Clarkson to the office. Roger came in and sat down. The Inspector began at once.

'Now, Mr Clarkson. Why was your mother angry with you last night?'

'This house is very big,' Roger said. 'It was a lot of work for Mother. I wanted her to move. But no, she loved this house and garden. She didn't want to move.'

'Tell me about your job, Mr Clarkson. Your mother is dead and now you're rich. Do you need money?'

'I need money, that's true.'

Roger's face was suddenly afraid. 'What are you saying? I didn't kill my mother. I need money, that's true. A friend and I want to build ten houses here, in this garden. We can get a lot of money for them. So I wanted Mother to sell this house. It's true. But Mr Briggs wanted half the garden, too, you know, for his farm.'

Inspector Walsh moved a pencil on the table. 'Tell me, what happened upstairs? You went to your mother's room?'

'Yes, I did. I wanted to say goodnight to my mother.'

'Did you talk about the house again?'

'Yes, I did. Again, she said no. She loved the house and didn't want to sell it.'

Inspector Walsh watched Roger for a minute. 'I see. We found the empty bottle of sleeping tablets, Mr Clarkson, in Diane's room.'

Roger's face did not change. 'Oh? Someone put them there. Diane did not kill my mother, I know that. She found the body.'

'Very well. I would like to see Diane next.'

Roger got up and left the room.

Inspector Walsh stood up and put his hands in his pockets. He went to the window and looked out at the trees. Why was Roger Clarkson afraid? Was it important? He looked at Sergeant Foster.

'Tomorrow morning, go to Mr Clarkson's office –

you have the name,' he said. 'Ask some questions about him, about his job, friends, money.'

Sergeant Foster wrote it down. 'Yes, Inspector.'

'A good day for tennis, Sergeant?'

Sergeant Foster laughed. 'Don't say that. It's not easy, you know. I don't like sitting here looking at the sun.'

Diane came into the room and sat down. She looked at Sergeant Foster and smiled. 'I saw you at the Tennis Club last month, I think. You play very well.'

Sergeant Foster's face went red. Inspector Walsh looked at him. 'Oh yes. A fast and exciting player is Sergeant Foster.'

Diane smiled again at Sergeant Foster and his face went redder.

'Well, Miss Clarkson,' Inspector Walsh said, 'I want you to talk about last night.'

Diane stopped smiling. 'Oh, I can talk about last night. I can't stop talking about it. We were all angry. Mother went to bed early and I made hot milk for her. We were all in the kitchen, and Peter Hobbs came in. He nearly broke the back door down.' Diane stopped.

'Yes?'

'He was very angry about a letter. He wanted to kill Mother. Are you going to talk to him?'

'We're going to talk to everyone.'

'Good. Tom Briggs came into the kitchen, too. Are you going to talk to him?'

'Peter Hobbs was very angry about a letter.'

'I'm asking the questions, Miss Clarkson. When did you take the milk upstairs?'

'I went up after Roger.' She stopped for a minute. Then she began again. 'I didn't like my mother, Inspector. She killed my father, you know. Last winter, after Christmas, she drove the car into a tree and killed my father.'

Inspector Walsh watched Diane's face carefully. 'I see. So you wanted to kill your mother?'

Diane laughed. 'I wanted to kill her, but I didn't. I can tell you a lot of things about this family, Inspector. Everyone wanted Mother to die. Uncle Albert wanted her money for his wife, Annie. And then my brother.

He needs a lot of money. He has an expensive house and an expensive car. And think of Jackie. Do you know that Jackie didn't like Mother? A long time ago, a nice boy worked here. He was the gardener. Jackie loved him very much, but Mother said no. A gardener was not a good husband for a Clarkson girl!'

Inspector Walsh listened quietly. All this was very interesting but was it important? Perhaps. What a happy family the Clarksons were!

'We found the empty bottle of sleeping tablets in your room,' Inspector Walsh said quietly. He watched her face carefully.

Diane stood up suddenly, her face angry. 'What? I didn't put it there! I'm not going to listen to this!' She ran out of the room.

'Well, well, well,' Inspector Walsh said. 'She likes you, Sergeant. You need to be careful.'

Sergeant Foster laughed but his face went red again.

'Someone put sleeping tablets in Molly's hot milk,' the Inspector said. 'All the family were in the kitchen last night. Peter Hobbs and Tom Briggs were there, too. One of them killed Molly.'

Inspector Walsh got his hat and coat. 'Come on. We need to talk to Peter Hobbs and Tom Briggs. Let's get some more coffee first. I'd like a sandwich, too. I'm hungry again!'

Chapter 6

They found Peter Hobbs under his car – an old green car. He got up slowly. He wore old blue trousers and a dirty orange shirt.

'We want to talk about Mrs Clarkson,' Inspector Walsh said.

'Oh, it's about her,' Peter said. He looked at the Inspector. 'I know she's dead. Someone in the village told me.'

'Why did you go to the Clarksons' house last night?'

'Jackie wanted me to come and see her brother, Roger. "You're angry," she said. "Come and tell Roger." I went to the house but nobody opened the door. So I made a lot of noise and then they opened the door. Old Mrs Clarkson wasn't there. But I told Roger. I told them all!' Peter hit the car with his hand. 'I wanted to kill that woman. I lost my job, my first job, because of her. Last month I was in trouble with the police and that old woman wrote to my office and she told them about the police. I wanted to kill her!'

'Take it easy!' Inspector Walsh said. 'What happened next?'

'Jackie gave me some coffee, but her brother didn't listen to me,' Peter said angrily. 'Then Tom Briggs

'*I wanted to kill that woman.*'

came in. He wanted to talk to Roger, too. But Roger didn't listen to him. Jackie was very unhappy – she nearly cried. Then I went home. That's all.'

'I see. Now tell me about the tablets. You went to the village on Thursday?'

'Tablets? Oh, yes. I remember. Jackie wanted me to get her mother's tablets from the village. I go to the village on my bicycle – this car doesn't work.'

'Thank you, Peter. That's all.'

'That's all?' Peter laughed angrily. 'You're going to come back, I know that! I know the police!'

Tom Briggs' farm was about half a mile away, near the

Tom Briggs' farm was not big, and the house was old and dirty.

river. It was not a big farm, and the house was old and dirty.

'Not much money here,' Inspector Walsh said.

Tom Briggs was a young man, about thirty years old, with dirty hands and bad teeth. 'What's wrong? Excuse me, I'm eating my dinner,' he said.

'We can wait. Finish your dinner,' Inspector Walsh said. 'We want to ask one or two questions about last night.'

'Come and wait in the front room,' Tom said and opened the door.

Inspector Walsh looked at the things in the front room. There was an old black and white television, and some books on the table. There was a picture of a happy young girl with long brown hair on the table, too. Inspector Walsh looked at the picture for a long time. Who was the girl?

Tom Briggs came back into the front room.

'Finished?' Inspector Walsh asked. 'You know Mrs Clarkson is dead?'

Tom Briggs sat down suddenly on the nearest chair. 'What? How did she die? When did it happen? I was there last night.'

'She died last night or early this morning. What did you do last night?'

'Me? Why are you asking me? I went there to meet Mr Clarkson – Roger. I'm losing money on this farm and I need more land. I want half Mrs Clarkson's garden.'

'You went into the kitchen. What did you do next? Can you remember?'

Tom Briggs looked at Sergeant Foster and then back at Inspector Walsh. 'I remember it very well. All the family were in the kitchen. Peter Hobbs was there, too. I talked to Roger. He wants his mother to sell the house. But *he* wants the land. He doesn't want me to have it. But now Mrs Clarkson is dead. What's going to happen now?'

Inspector Walsh got up and took the picture of the girl from the table. 'Who's this?'

Tom's face went red. 'It's not . . . It was a long time ago.'

Tom's face went red. 'Who? Oh! That's a friend. It's not . . . It was a long time ago.'

The two detectives walked back to the Clarksons' house through the garden. It was beautiful, green and quiet. Inspector Walsh felt tired and hungry. Who killed Molly? He knew the answer now, but he needed to ask one or two more questions.

'Let's go, Sergeant,' he said, and put on his hat again. 'Tomorrow is a new day.'

Chapter 7

O n Monday morning Sergeant Foster went to
Roger's office and asked some questions. And
then he went to Albert's house and asked some more
questions. Inspector Walsh sat in his office and
telephoned. He made phone calls about Peter Hobbs
and he made phone calls about Tom Briggs. And then
he had some coffee and sandwiches.

At three o'clock the two detectives drove to the
Clarksons' house.

The two detectives drove to the Clarksons' house.

'I would like to see everyone,' he told Roger.

Everyone came into the sitting room and sat down.

Inspector Walsh stood in front of the windows and looked at them, one by one. 'I want to talk to you. Someone killed Molly Clarkson. Someone put sleeping tablets in her hot milk and killed her. Nobody wanted to tell me the true story, but now I know the true story and I'm going to tell you.'

The two dogs came slowly into the room and sat down at Diane's feet. It was very quiet in the room.

The Inspector looked at Albert. 'Mr King, your wife is very ill and needs a nurse. You told me this. You didn't tell me about your house. You're selling your house next month because you need the money.'

Albert was angry. 'Last year I asked Molly's husband for some money, and he said yes. But then he died in an accident.'

'Accident!' Diane cried. 'That was no accident. Mother killed Daddy because she wanted his money!'

'Let's talk about you now, Diane,' said Inspector Walsh. 'You visited your mother every month and you took money from her. Last month she gave you money for your television. This month she gave you money for your telephone. Every month you told your mother: "It was no accident; you killed Daddy. I'm going to tell the police." Your mother was afraid of the police and so she gave you the money. But in the end she wanted

'Now I know the true story . . .'

to stop you. She told Dr Pratt. No more money, she told Dr Pratt on Thursday; and on Saturday she died. You took the hot milk to your mother – what did she tell you?'

Diane began to cry. 'I loved Daddy! He always gave money to me; he loved me. It was Mother – she didn't love Daddy and she didn't love me.' Diane stopped. The dogs got up and went to the door. 'It's true, I took a lot of money from Mother. On Saturday she told me – no more money. I wanted to kill her, but I didn't.'

The dogs came back and sat down again at Diane's feet.

Inspector Walsh looked at Roger. 'Mr Clarkson also needed money.'

Roger's face went red. 'Don't tell them! Please!'

'Mr Clarkson lost his job last month. He has no money. But he has an expensive house and an expensive car. He likes expensive things.'

His sisters looked at him, but Roger put his hand over his eyes. 'Don't talk to me!'

'It doesn't matter now!' Diane said. 'Mother is dead and we have a lot of money. You don't need a job.'

Roger's face went red again. 'Be quiet, Diane!'

'Now,' Inspector Walsh began again. 'Peter Hobbs is a very angry young man. Mrs Clarkson was not very nice to him. He got the sleeping tablets from the shop. But did he put the tablets in the hot milk? I think not.

Tom Briggs wanted half the garden for his farm. He was in the kitchen that night. Did he put sleeping tablets in the hot milk? I think not.'

Suddenly it began to rain. For a minute everyone watched it through the window. Jackie took a cigarette from her bag and began to smoke.

'But someone wanted Peter Hobbs to come into the kitchen that night. She wanted everyone to see him, and listen to him,' Inspector Walsh said.

'She . . . ? I don't understand,' Roger began, and stopped.

Inspector Walsh moved away from the window and sat down. 'I'm going to tell you the true story now. Miss Clarkson, you wanted Peter Hobbs to come to the house that night. He was very angry with your mother because of that letter. He said: "I want to kill her." And you wanted everyone to hear that. Why?'

Jackie's face went white. 'It's not true! What about Diane? You found the empty bottle in her bag!'

Diane stood up. 'In my bag? Jackie! What are you talking about?'

'Be quiet, please, and sit down,' Inspector Walsh said. He looked at Jackie. 'It's true: we found the bottle in Diane's bag. But how do you know that? We didn't tell you.'

'You did . . . before . . . you told me before!'

'No. We found the empty bottle in Diane's *room.*

*Jackie asked, 'What about Diane? You found the empty
bottle in her bag.'*

We told you that. You talked about Diane's bag; we
didn't tell you. Sergeant Foster wrote it all down.'
Inspector Walsh looked carefully at Jackie. 'A long
time ago, you knew Tom Briggs. He was the gardener
here and you loved him. But your mother didn't like
him.'

Jackie put her hands to her head. 'No! No!'

'We found your picture – an old one – in Mr Briggs'
house. You were younger then, and your hair was
long. Last year Tom Briggs came back, and you
wanted him. He loved you, too, but he had no money.
He wanted the garden for his farm, he wanted money,

he wanted you. But your mother said no. In the end, you wanted to kill your mother . . . and you did kill her. Your mother went downstairs to see the dogs and you put the sleeping tablets in her hot milk. Later, you put the empty bottle in Diane's bag.'

Jackie stood up. Her eyes were dark and afraid. 'You don't understand!' she cried. 'Mother gave me nothing . . . all those years. I wanted to be happy . . . to be with Tom. That's all. I love Tom, and he loves me. But Mother said no. Always no.' Then she began to cry. Nobody looked at her.

Jackie left the house in a police car. Inspector Walsh watched and then walked slowly to his car. He felt tired and hungry. He stopped and looked back at the house.

'Well,' he said to Sergeant Foster, 'in the end, they got the money: Albert, Roger, Diane. They're all rich now. But are they going to be happy?'

He got into the car. 'Let's go,' he said. 'I'm hungry; I need a sandwich.'

GLOSSARY

aunt   the sister of your father or mother, or the wife of your uncle

build   to make a house or a building

club   a number of people who meet because they are interested in the same thing (e.g. a tennis club)

cup   a thing to put drinks in

empty   with nothing in it

farm *(n)*   land and buildings where people grow things to eat and keep animals for food

find out   to ask questions and learn about something

inspector   an important policeman or policewoman

job   when you work and get money for it, you have a job

kitchen   a room where people make breakfast, dinner, etc.

land *(n)*   ground (not water – sea, rivers, etc.)

lie *(v)*   to say something that is not true

murder *(n)*   killing somebody (not in an accident)

murderer   somebody who murders

police   people who look for bad people

ring (past tense **rang**)   to make a sound like a bell (e.g. a telephone rings)

sell   to give something to someone and they give you money for it

sergeant   a policeman or policewoman

tablet   a doctor gives you tablets to eat and you feel better

trouble *(n)*   something bad, or difficult, or unhappy

uncle   the brother of your mother or father, or the husband of your aunt

wine   a cold drink made from grapes

ACTIVITIES

Before Reading

1 **Read the back cover of the book. How much do you know now about the story? Choose Y (yes) or N (no) each time.**

1 Molly Clarkson is fifteen years old. Y/N *N*
2 Molly is having a small party. Y/N *N*
3 The four people at the party need Molly's money. Y/N *Y*
4 Someone is going to kill Molly. Y/N *Y*

2 **Now read the introduction on the first page of the book. Are you a good detective? Choose Y (yes) or N (no).**

1 Inspector Walsh works quickly. Y/N *N*
2 A detective looks for clues. Y/N *N*
3 A good clue stops the killer. Y/N *N*
4 There are no clues in this story. Y/N *N*
5 The killer is going to lie. Y/N *Y*

3 **Can you answer these questions about detective stories?**

1 Do you know any famous detectives from stories in films or on television? What were their names? *No, I don't know*
2 Does the detective always catch the murderer? *No.*
3 Is 'Love or Money?' a good title for a detective story? What does it tell you about the story?
   No. love important than money.

ACTIVITIES

While Reading

Read Chapter 1, then answer these questions.

1 Who had no money for the train ticket? *Diane*

2 Why was Jackie angry with her sister? *Because Diane always want money from her mother*

3 What did Molly want Jackie to do? *he go to the village and get the*

4 Why was Peter Hobbs very angry with Molly?
Because make it lose his work

Read Chapter 2. Who said these words in the chapter?

1 'She needs a nurse twenty-four hours a day.' *Albert*

2 'All your things are expensive.' *Jeakie*

3 'It's a lot of work for you. The house is big, too.' *Roger*

4 'Nobody is getting more money from me.' *Molly*

5 'One day I'm going to kill that woman.' *Daine Diane*

Read Chapter 3, then answer these questions.

Who

1 . . . found Molly's body? *Diane*

2 . . . heard a cry from Molly's room? *Roger*

3 . . . phoned the doctor? *Bb Diane*

4 . . . took sleeping tablets? *Juokie*

5 . . . looked for the bottle of sleeping tablets in the room? *Roger*

6 . . . phoned the police? *Roger*

Before you read Chapter 4, can you guess the murderer's name? Put P (perhaps) or N (no) by these names.

Uncle Albert   Jackie Clarkson   Peter Hobbs

Diane Clarkson   Roger Clarkson   Tom Briggs

Read Chapters 4 and 5. Here are some untrue sentences about the chapters. Change them into true sentences.

1 Somebody put sleeping tablets in Roger's coffee. *Molly*

2 Nobody saw Molly in her room that night. *Somebody*

3 Albert needed money because he was ill. *were*

4 Jackie made hot milk and took it to Diane. *Molly*

5 At midnight Jackie went downstairs to see the dogs. *Diane lose*

6 Peter Hobbs found his job because of Molly. *lose*

7 Roger did not want his mother to sell the house.

8 Diane loved her mother. *do not*

Read Chapter 6. Peter Hobbs and Tom Briggs said these things to Inspector Walsh. Who said what?

1 'What? How did she die? When did it happen?' *Briggs*

2 'I know she's dead. Someone in the village told me.' *Hobbs*

3 'That old woman wrote to my office.' *Hobbs*

4 'I want half Mrs Clarkson's garden.' *Briggs*

5 'I wanted to kill that woman.' *Hobbs*

6 'Who? Oh! That's a friend. It was a long time ago.' *Briggs*

Before you read Chapter 7, can you name the murderer?
Write P (perhaps), N (no), or Y (yes) by the names.

Uncle Albert   Roger Clarkson   Peter Hobbs
Diane Clarkson   Jackie Clarkson   Tom Briggs

Read Chapter 7. Before they got to the house, Sergeant
Foster asked Inspector Walsh some questions. Match the
right answer to each question.

Sergeant Foster's questions
  1 'Why is Albert King selling his house?'
  2 'Tom Briggs didn't do it. So why is he important?'
  3 'Diane visited her mother every month and took
     money from her. How do we know that?'
  4 'And Roger – why does he want to build houses?'
  5 'What about Jackie? Does she need money?'
  6 'Did the angry young man, Peter Hobbs, do it?'
  7 'So who *did* put those tablets in the hot milk?'
Inspector Walsh's answers
  8 'Because Mrs Clarkson told Dr Pratt, and he told me.'
  9 'No. He talked a lot about killing, but he didn't do it.'
  10 'Because he needs the money for a nurse for his wife.'
  11 'No, she doesn't need money. She needs love.'
  12 'Come on, Sergeant – you tell me!'
  13 'Because he lost his job last month and needs money.'
  14 'He's important because he was the Clarksons'
     gardener many years ago.'

ACTIVITIES

After Reading

1 Match the people with the sentences. Then use the sentences
   to write about the people. Use pronouns (*he, she, him*) and
   linking words (*and, but, so*).

Molly / Jackie / Diane / Roger / Albert
Example: *Molly was fifty years old **and** was very rich.*
She . . .

1 *Molly* was fifty years old.
2 *Jackie* wanted to marry Tom Briggs but Molly said no.
3 *Diane* was a good singer but could never get work.
4 *Roger* lived in an expensive house.
5 *Albert*'s wife was Molly's sister.
6 *Jackie* killed Molly with sleeping tablets in hot milk.
7 *Molly* was very rich.
8 *Molly* didn't want to sell his house.
9 *Diane* always got money from her father.
10 *Roger* lost his job last month.
11 *Albert* needed the money for his sick wife.
12 *Molly* didn't like Tom Briggs.
13 *Diane* was very sorry when her father died.
14 *Jackie* put the empty bottle in Diane's bag.
15 *Molly* didn't want Jackie to marry Tom Briggs.
16 *Briggs* wanted to build houses in Molly's garden.

2 This conversation between Diane and Molly happened after the dinner, in Molly's room. The conversation is in the wrong order. Write it out in the correct order and put in the speakers' names. Diane speaks first (number 5).

B 1 Molly 'Thank you. Where are my sleeping tablets?'

D 2 Molly 'Well, I don't want to talk. I'm not going to give you more money, Diane.'

3 Diane 'Yes, you did. You wanted his money. I heard you at Christmas when you told Aunt Annie that. I'm going to talk to her about it.'

4 Diane 'An accident! No, Mother. Why did you hit that tree? It was daytime and you're a good driver.'

A 5 Diane 'Here's your hot milk, Mother.'

6 Diane 'Oh yes, you are! Or do you want me to talk to the police about Daddy? You wanted to kill him, I know.'

7 Molly 'Good drivers can have accidents too, you know. Listen, Diane, it was an accident. How many times must I tell you? I was angry with Daddy, but I didn't want to kill him.'

C 8 Diane 'Here's the bottle, on your table. No, don't open your book. I want to talk to you about money.'

9 Molly 'I didn't want to kill him, Diane! It was an accident!'

F 10 Diane 'Please don't do that! Annie is very ill!'

3 **Choose a good (G) title for each chapter. One heading is not good (NG). Explain why.**

Chapter 1 The Hottest Day of the Year NG

The Clarkson Family G

Diane Needs Money

Chapter 2 Molly Says No NG

A Wonderful Dress

A Birthday Dinner G

Chapter 3 Dr Pratt Phones the Police

The Bottle of Sleeping Tablets G

Diane and the Dogs NG

Chapter 4 Sergeant Foster and the Tennis Club

The Police Ask Questions NG

A Cup of Hot Milk G

Chapter 5 I Didn't Kill My Mother NG

Sergeant Foster and Diane

An Old Love Story G

Chapter 6 The Picture of a Friend G

Inspector Walsh Feels Hungry NG

Inspector Walsh Knows the Answer

Chapter 7 Mother Gave Me Nothing NG

Love and Money G

Accident!

4 Here is a new illustration for the story. Answer these
  questions about the illustration.

1 Who is the girl on the stairs and what is she doing?
  Diane, she is going to give molly coffe.
2 Who are the other two people in this picture?
  Jackie, Roger Albert
3 Where is Albert?
  Near the door
4 What happened next? Write three or four sentences.

Now write a caption for the illustration.

Caption: _____

5 **What happened next? Here are five different endings. Fill in the gaps with these words. (Use each word once.) Which ending or endings do you like best?**

didn't, farm, garden, happy, house, love, love, love, married, money, money, money, murder, never, nobody, rich

1 Jackie went to prison for the _____ of her mother and at first _____ visited her. In the end Roger and Diane went to see her, but they _____ talk about Molly.

2 After ten years Jackie came out of prison and _____ Tom Briggs. They lived very quietly and they didn't have much _____, but they were _____.

3 Roger lived in Molly's _____. He built ten houses in the _____ and was soon a very _____ man. Diane found a husband, but she didn't _____ him. She married him because he had a lot of _____.

4 Jackie _____ saw Tom Briggs again because he sold his _____ to Roger and went to live in Australia. Jackie never married, and so she never found _____.

5 The Clarkson family are nicer people now. After their mother died, they learnt something – they learnt that _____ is more important than _____.

ABOUT THE AUTHOR

Rowena Akinyemi is British, and after many years in Africa, she now lives and works in Cambridge. She has worked in English Language Teaching for twenty years, in Africa and England, and has been writing ELT fiction for ten years. *Love or Money?* was her first story for the Oxford Bookworms Library, and she has now written several other stories for the series, including *Remember Miranda* and *The Witches of Pendle* (both at Stage 1). She has also written books for children. One of her favourite pastimes is reading detective stories.

OXFORD BOOKWORMS LIBRARY

Classics • Crime & Mystery • Factfiles • Fantasy & Horror
Human Interest • Playscripts • Thriller & Adventure
True Stories • World Stories

The OXFORD BOOKWORMS LIBRARY provides enjoyable reading in English, with a wide range of classic and modern fiction, non-fiction, and plays. It includes original and adapted texts in seven carefully graded language stages, which take learners from beginner to advanced level. An overview is given on the next pages.

All Stage 1 titles are available as audio recordings, as well as over eighty other titles from Starter to Stage 6. All Starters and many titles at Stages 1 to 4 are specially recommended for younger learners. Every Bookworm is illustrated, and Starters and Factfiles have full-colour illustrations.

The OXFORD BOOKWORMS LIBRARY also offers extensive support. Each book contains an introduction to the story, notes about the author, a glossary, and activities. Additional resources include tests and worksheets, and answers for these and for the activities in the books. There is advice on running a class library, using audio recordings, and the many ways of using Oxford Bookworms in reading programmes. Resource materials are available on the website <www.oup.com/elt/gradedreaders>.

The *Oxford Bookworms Collection* is a series for advanced learners. It consists of volumes of short stories by well-known authors, both classic and modern. Texts are not abridged or adapted in any way, but carefully selected to be accessible to the advanced student.

You can find details and a full list of titles in the *Oxford Bookworms Library Catalogue* and *Oxford English Language Teaching Catalogues*, and on the website <www.oup.com/elt/gradedreaders>.

THE OXFORD BOOKWORMS LIBRARY
GRADING AND SAMPLE EXTRACTS

STARTER • 250 HEADWORDS

present simple – present continuous – imperative –
can/*cannot*, *must* – *going to* (future) – simple gerunds …

Her phone is ringing – but where is it?

Sally gets out of bed and looks in her bag. No phone. She looks under the bed. No phone. Then she looks behind the door. There is her phone. Sally picks up her phone and answers it. *Sally's Phone*

STAGE 1 • 400 HEADWORDS

… past simple – coordination with *and*, *but*, *or* –
subordination with *before*, *after*, *when*, *because*, *so* …

I knew him in Persia. He was a famous builder and I worked with him there. For a time I was his friend, but not for long. When he came to Paris, I came after him – I wanted to watch him. He was a very clever, very dangerous man. *The Phantom of the Opera*

STAGE 2 • 700 HEADWORDS

… present perfect – *will* (future) – *(don't) have to*, *must not*, *could* –
comparison of adjectives – simple *if* clauses – past continuous –
tag questions – *ask*/*tell* + infinitive …

While I was writing these words in my diary, I decided what to do. I must try to escape. I shall try to get down the wall outside. The window is high above the ground, but I have to try. I shall take some of the gold with me – if I escape, perhaps it will be helpful later. *Dracula*

STAGE 3 • 1000 HEADWORDS

... should, may – present perfect continuous – *used to* – past perfect –
causative – relative clauses – indirect statements ...

Of course, it was most important that no one should see
Colin, Mary, or Dickon entering the secret garden. So Colin
gave orders to the gardeners that they must all keep away
from that part of the garden in future. *The Secret Garden*

STAGE 4 • 1400 HEADWORDS

... past perfect continuous – passive (simple forms) –
would conditional clauses – indirect questions –
relatives with *where/when* – gerunds after prepositions/phrases ...

I was glad. Now Hyde could not show his face to the world
again. If he did, every honest man in London would be proud
to report him to the police. *Dr Jekyll and Mr Hyde*

STAGE 5 • 1800 HEADWORDS

... future continuous – future perfect –
passive (modals, continuous forms) –
would have conditional clauses – modals + perfect infinitive ...

If he had spoken Estella's name, I would have hit him. I was so
angry with him, and so depressed about my future, that I could
not eat the breakfast. Instead I went straight to the old house.
Great Expectations

STAGE 6 • 2500 HEADWORDS

... passive (infinitives, gerunds) – advanced modal meanings –
clauses of concession, condition

When I stepped up to the piano, I was confident. It was as if I
knew that the prodigy side of me really did exist. And when I
started to play, I was so caught up in how lovely I looked that
I didn't worry how I would sound. *The Joy Luck Club*

BOOKWORMS · CRIME & MYSTERY · STAGE 1

Sherlock Holmes and the Sport of Kings

SIR ARTHUR CONAN DOYLE
Retold by Jennifer Bassett

Horseracing is the sport of kings, perhaps because racehorses are very expensive animals. But when they win races, they can make a lot of money too – money for the owners, for the trainers, and for the people who put bets on them to win.

Silver Blaze is a young horse, but already the winner of many races. One night he disappears from his stables, and someone kills his trainer. The police want the killer, and the owner wants his horse, but they can't find them. So what do they do?

They write to 221B Baker Street, London, of course – to ask for the help of the great detective, Sherlock Holmes.

BOOKWORMS · TRUE STORIES · STAGE 1

Ned Kelly: A True Story

CHRISTINE LINDOP

When he was a boy, he was poor and hungry. When he was a young man, he was still poor and still hungry. He learnt how to steal horses, he learnt how to fight, he learnt how to live – outside the law. Australia in the 1870s was a hard, wild place. Rich people had land, poor people didn't. So the rich got richer, and the poor stayed poor.

Some say Ned Kelly was a bad man. Some say he was a good man but the law was bad. This is the true story of Australia's most famous outlaw.